THE STARTING GUIDE

YOUR FIRST
MOBILE
APP
+
BUSINESS
101 TIPS

SHEENA ALLEN

www.SheenaAllen.co

ISBN 978-0-9987166-0-2

First Edition

"Don't focus so much on proving the doubters wrong. Stay focused and work to prove yourself right."

- Sheena Allen

The Starting Guide is dedicated to everyone stepping outside of his or her comfort zone. The challenge and reward awaits.

 www.SheenaAllen.co

 @whoisSheena

 @whoisSheena

 @whoisSheena

 /SheenaDAllen

Contents

Part 1
The Personal Journey
11

Part 2
Creating a Mobile App with No Coding Skills
25

The Why - Part I

I find myself laughing every time I am around my little nephew and he asks question after question. Sometimes, our conversations can go like this:

> Khaleb: "Why do I have to wear a jacket?
> Me: "Because it is cold."
> Khaleb: "Why is it cold?"
> Me: "Because it is winter time."
> Khaleb: "Why is it winter time?"
> Me: "Because that's the season we are in."

It usually doesn't stop there, but for the sake of this introduction, I will. Plus, I am sure there was a point in my life when I asked "why?" of everything someone told me, too. Amazingly enough, I have found that asking "why?" when it comes to business can be a valuable habit. Asking "why?" at least three times let's us know if we truly understand the purpose of why we are pursuing our chosen business venture. When I attended a Google for Entrepreneurs program at the American Underground in Durham, North Carolina in 2016, one of the advisors asked me why I started CapWay. I answered. He followed my answer by asking "why?" again. I answered. After that, he asked me "why?" for a third time. I soon realized he wanted to know if I truly knew the purpose of my company.

If you are wondering why you should read this book instead of the many other books and articles available to teach you and give you tips about how to create a mobile app, know that my personal journey makes a difference. Why? My failures and successes through trial and error give me insights and lessons that I can pass on to you that others may not be able to. Why? I didn't attend an Ivy League school, I didn't know how to code, and I didn't have family and friends that were rich enough to fund my "family and friends" round of funding. Therefore, the tips and suggestions that I am going to share with you come from experiences I have had, and some lessons I have learned the hard way. I am more like you than you may think. That is what makes this book different.

My mentors always tell me "each one, teach one." I wrote this book to help guide you and give you the motivation and inspiration to go out and get it done. Whatever it may be. Know that it is possible to do whatever you set your mind to.

Now, let's get it done!

Part 1
The Personal Journey

The Magic in Youth

I was born and raised in Terry, Mississippi, a small, country town that is located on the outskirts of the capital city of Jackson. When I say small, I do mean small. The population is barely over 1,000 and we do not have any stoplights, only stop signs.

Even though I didn't fall in love with technology until college, I was always a lover of weird and different things. I thank God for parents that allowed me to express myself in numerous creative ways without judging me or telling me how I should do things as I was growing up. One of my first loves was drawing and painting. I wanted to grow up to be an artist. While most kids draw on paper, I was drawing on paper, plus my bedroom walls and any other medium that was available. I remember taking a day to draw and paint Disney characters all over my bedroom walls without asking my parents for their permission. When my mom came to my room, she didn't fuss. Neither did my dad. I won't say that they were happy about it, but they were all for me expressing myself in whatever crazy and creative way I thought of. In fact, they never put me in a box or steered me to follow a path that they wanted for me. They pushed my brother and me to make mistakes, learn from them, and follow the path in life that makes us happy.

Although I'm only in my twenties now, I look back and realize the magic in being young. The youth before I had to start adulting. What I wouldn't give to be able to take naps and go outside to recess and have no real worries! Kids are special because of their innocence. They just live. They don't overthink a situation and they're usually honest, even though you may not like what they have to say. For that reason, it is part of my routine during the development process to talk to kids. I value their feedback because I know their opinion is unfiltered. I can't go back to being five, but I try to hold on to a piece of kid inside of me. There is a beauty in coloring outside of the lines and there is magic in youth. We just have to find that magic as adults too.

College Changed My Life

After graduating from Terry High School in 2007, I went on to attend the University of Southern Mississippi where I double majored in Psychology and Film, with a minor in Marketing. My original plan for life as a college freshman was to be an Industrial/Organizational (I/O) psychologist that would write and direct movies, TV shows, and music videos in my spare time. I wanted to bring back the storytelling to music videos; a return to how Michael Jackson's videos used to be. As weird and crazy as that sounds now, it was really my life plan at 18 and 19.

Before college, I changed my plans more than once. In the early years of high school, I wanted to be an artist, but everyone told me that would equate to me working on my art part-time and working as a bartender or waitress the rest of my time because being an artist doesn't pay. At sixteen that sounded terrifying, so I shifted my plans. Next up, I was going to be a pharmacist. I really had no reason why other than I knew that it was good pay and that I couldn't be a doctor because the sight of blood or anything gruesome makes me light-headed and nauseated. So being a pharmacist it was.

As much trouble as I was having deciding on a major, I had the same trouble trying to decide what college I would attend. My top choice was Louisiana State University (LSU), but after I didn't get a full scholarship, I made the decision to just focus on the colleges that did give me a scholarship. At no point during my thought process did I think about the true advantages and disadvantages of attending a particular university. For example, the network that comes with being Stanford, Harvard, or Howard alumni can work magic for you in ways that networks from smaller colleges cannot.

I ended up at the University of Southern Mississippi (USM), about an hour and a half from home. Unsure of what I was getting myself into in fall 2007, I look back now and know that college changed my life. USM changed my life. Unexpectedly, the disadvantage of going to a college that doesn't focus on technology gave me an advantage when I started my journey. A trip to Wal-Mart in 2011 during my senior year of college spurred my journey to begin.

My roommate and I took a trip to Wal-Mart to stock up on personal and household supplies for our apartment. After leaving, I was left with a long receipt and I told my roommate, "It would be so cool if there was an app that I could use to help me keep up with my money and my receipts." Mind you, I had no technical background. Owning an iPhone and having a few apps on my phone was as good as it got for me. However, I had made it up in my mind that I was going to create this financial

16

mobile application. Once we returned to our apartment, I went to my computer, opened Microsoft Word and started to design and write out the functionality of this app that I had just thought of. I didn't know the proper software program to use, but I knew that I could use the text boxes in Microsoft Word to resemble the screen of an iPhone. I did not really know where to start, but I knew that if I was going to find a developer to help me, I wanted him/her to know and understand the design and specifications of the functions of the app that I wanted to create. Once done in Microsoft Word, I created and completed a flowchart, although at the time I didn't know that was what I was doing. I was just doing what made sense to me. After finishing my flow chart, I went to Google.com to search for an app developer. I came across guru.com, where I found a developer to partner with to code my first app. With a $3,500 loan from my dad, I went from an idea to an actual product. With that, at the age of 22 and a senior in college, my business baby was born. Sheena Allen Apps gave birth to its firth brainchild, a finance app called PAMO.

I graduated from USM in December 2011 and was very unsure of where I was headed. I had fallen in love with technology and I wanted to pursue building Sheena Allen Apps to be the tech company I knew it could be. My dad was pushing me to get a job since I had two degrees. He often preached that I needed a job that guaranteed me a steady income, which is the opposite of entrepreneurship, especially in the early years of a startup. I had a choice to make. I was going to find a job to earn money until I started grad school or I was going to put my all into being an entrepreneur. I decided to give myself a year to follow my passion and give myself a fighting chance, even though I truly knew nothing about being an entrepreneur. I said that if I didn't find true success within one year, grad school it was.

In 2012, I saw a picture that a friend created in Photoshop that showed her playing basketball against herself. I thought it was the coolest thing I had ever seen. I wanted to be able to create photos like it. I wanted everyone to be able to create photos like it. I knew from the minute I saw her photo that a photo-editing program would be my next app - and I knew it was going to be a game changer. I worked with my developer for four or five months to perfect the app. In the summer of 2012, I released the app for iPhone and named it Dubblen. Dubblen ended up being the app that changed everything for me. It was the app that told me that technology and entrepreneurship was the right path for me. I went from a total of 5,000 downloads in 6 months in 2011 to 5,000 downloads a week after initially releasing Dubblen for iPhone. I would eventually go on to have 5,000+ a day as I continued building the company and adding more apps.

In 2013, the year that I could have potentially been starting grad school, I was instead releasing my first Android app. Dubblen was such a success on iOS that

Android users were demanding it. I released Dubblen for Android in early 2013 and people were downloading it at rate that I had never experienced before. After seeing those numbers, it was safe to say that I had found success. However, the success was bittersweet. I was building this app company with wonderful numbers in regards to downloads and retention, but no one was e-mailing me or knocking on my door to invest in my company. There weren't many investors in Mississippi. Even worse, there weren't any similar tech companies in Mississippi that I could go to for guidance. I was starting to feel stuck. I came to the conclusion that I needed to move away to a tech hub to truly build out Sheena Allen Apps to its full potential. Hot off of the release of Dubblen for Android and a little over a year after graduating from college, I made one of the biggest decisions of my life. I packed my bags and moved. Goodbye Mississippi.

Goodbye Mississippi

Before starting my tech company, I had never heard of Silicon Valley. But after I jumped into the world of app development, I heard and read about it all the time. The more research I did, the more it seemed to me that the place I had to be was Silicon Valley. I often say that going into this venture blind was my gift and my curse. It was my curse because I wasn't truly informed about anything. I didn't have any mentors or advisors. I was building a tech company without any true knowledge about the tech world. But going in blind was also my gift because I didn't overthink anything. I didn't know about the horrible stats of women and minorities in tech. I didn't know about the difficulty of raising money as a black, woman in tech. I just knew I had found a passion and I had found some success and I was going to continue to build on it.

My first day in Silicon Valley was amazing. I remember passing the companies that I only knew from using them online. PayPal, eBay, Google. It was so amazing and I felt like a kid in a candy store. I felt like I had finally found my home. However, that excitement didn't last too long. My first trip to the grocery store left me dumbfounded. Everything was so expensive compared to Mississippi. Although I expected the cost of living to be higher, I didn't expect it to pay $3.00 more for something as simple as peanuts. The reality of the situation was that I was a fresh college graduate running a startup, and I didn't have rich parents to support me during my starting phase. This in no way meant that I was going to give up on my dreams, but I was going to have to find an alternative route to get there.

In August 2013, I reached out to a man listed as a mentor on the website of Capital Factory, a business accelerator in Austin, Texas. Austin was in the South and closer to home. Even better, it was a growing tech hub and it wasn't nearly as expensive as Silicon Valley. I put my pride aside and did something that I had never done before. I decided to send a cold e-mail to someone that I didn't know to ask them to mentor me and guide me if I decided to move to Austin. It was the first time I had ever done anything like that, but I knew that all he could do was say yes, no, or not write back, so I decided to shoot my shot.

He wrote me back and told me that while he loved my story and what I had achieved so far, he couldn't really help me. However, he introduced me to someone that he believed could be a great help to me. The person he introduced me to was Josh Kerr, and it was an introduction that led to another step up the ladder.

After having a phone call, Josh asked me how soon could I get to Austin. We ended up setting a date within the next week or so. On the day I got to town, Josh had meetings set up for me from that morning until late that evening. He really showed me the possibilities of what could happen if I moved to Austin. I was sold. Within two weeks, I made the move to Austin, started my co-working membership at Capital Factory, and was being mentored by Josh Kerr and Jason Seats, who was the director of Techstar Austin at that time.

I stayed in Austin for a year and I can truly say that I learned a lot. It was the best move that I had made up to that time. I went to Austin still learning through my own experiences and via trial and error. I left with more knowledge, more contacts, and more confidence.

I left Mississippi to not only become a better entrepreneur, but to step outside of my comfort zone. There were times that I missed my family and wanted to give up and go back and get a 9-5 job, but in the end, the move from Mississippi to a tech hub was the best move I could have made.

Aspire to Inspire

Since starting my first app as a senior in college, Sheena Allen Apps has grown from one app to five apps with millions of downloads. The current five apps are **Dubblen**, a photo app with a split camera that allows you to clone yourself in fun and creative ways; **Orange Snap**, a filter application that allows you to add multiple filters to one photo; **PicSlit**, a grid app that slits your photos into squares for amazing Instagram banners; **TwtBooth**, a Twitter application that allows you to view media that is tweeted; and **Words on Pics**, a photo app that allows you to add photo captions, thought bubbles, and speech bubbles to your photos.

The very first app that I ever created, PAMO, was renamed as InstaFunds in 2013. In 2016, I completely pivoted and made the app its own financial technology company. I took some of the core components of the original 2011 version of PAMO, along with changes made in 2013 with InstaFunds, and combined those with what I saw as a major lack in serving the unbanked and underbanked market. The result was a new finance app that was launched as CapWay in late 2016 with the goal of creating a new banking standard for the 2.5 billion people in this world who do not use traditional banking.

As I have said before, I jumped into the tech world blind. I did not know anything about owning a mobile application company. I did not know the proper techniques, the who or what, or even where to begin. But this is what I wanted and I was willing to learn. I've taken on every challenge and I know that reaching new levels bring new devils. However, one of the most important things to me on this journey is to share what I've learned in hopes that it helps others avoid mistakes that could cost them time and money.

If starting this journey scares you, that is fine. As long as you don't let fear stop you, you will be okay. Technology has taken me places and given me opportunities that I never dreamed of as a kid. I've found myself featured in publications like *Black Enterprise* and *EBONY*. I am part of a documentary film, *She Started It*, which has been shown at numerous film festivals, universities, and other venues throughout the world. Oh, and I visited the White House. Tech got me there. Not only has tech allowed me to change the lives of others, it has given me the platform to branch out to other possibilities, like exploring entertainment, fashion, and so much more. Even if it is not tech, don't be afraid to take your life into your own hands on the strength of what you are passionate about.

I hope you close this book feeling motivated and inspired. I hope you close this book at the end ready to create the next big thing. When doubting yourself, think back to the lyrics of the late Aaliyah. "If at first you don't succeed, dust yourself off and try again."

Part 2

Creating a Mobile App with No Coding Skills

The Idea

Every single day, my inbox is full of e-mails from people telling me the same thing: "I have an idea for an app, but I have no idea where to start." Everything starts with an idea and an idea can come to us at anytime. I've had them while traveling, while lying in bed, or while playing with my nieces and nephews.

You must note that the tech world moves fast. The same wonderful idea that you have so does two or three others. The differentiator in those with similar ideas is timing and execution. Some people can sit on an idea for years and never see anything like it come to the mass market. Others can have a great idea and not execute and will see that same idea result in a multi-million dollar company for someone else. If you don't act on your idea, I can guarantee you that someone else will.

One of the things that I had to learn was that not all good ideas equal a good business. There is a difference. However, in order to know if your idea could equate to a good business or not, you need to do some research. Are there already 20 apps similar to the one you want to create? This is important to know because you want to know what kind of competition you are going up against. If after doing your research, you still want to move forward with your idea, get your idea out of your head and on paper. Why? You may forget something, or better yet, you may want to expand your idea over time.

Getting it out of your head and on paper is also a learning exercise for you. I once had someone tell me after we worked through his idea together that the idea sounded much better in his head. No worries, it happens. Getting it out of your head and on paper enables you to see some of the holes in your idea. Trust me, there is beauty in the process, but it is indeed a process.

It is important to not let others discourage you and drive you away from the idea that you have. Truth is, it may work and it may not work, but just because someone else thinks that it is a stupid idea and won't work doesn't mean they are right. On the other hand, be very careful when walking that thin line between being an optimist and being a realist.

Search the Market

If you are serious about moving forward with your app idea, you need to do a quick search of the App Store to see if there are similar apps already available. Why? You need to know what you are up against. Are there two apps that are similar to what you want to create or are there 20 apps that would be considered competitors? How many apps similar to your idea have failed? Why did the app(s) fail? What is the market size for what you are trying to create? Is your market 1,000 people or 100,000 people or 1,000,000+ people? I will give you an example. If your app's primary audience is college graduates in the United States, you need to know that market. How many college students graduate per year in the United States? Whatever number that is, that is your market size.

Research. Research. Research. I am not talking about that high school or college English paper type of research. I'm talking about that "is my great idea a great idea that is already available on the market and being dominated by five other companies already" type of research. But with that said, let me add that just because an idea similar to yours is already available does not mean that you should give up on getting your app developed. What it does mean is that now you have to figure out a twist that will make your app better than the competitor's app. Think about it this way. How many different tablets are there available for you to purchase? Honestly, all tablets pretty much do the same thing. So, if you own a tablet, what was it about that tablet that made you purchase it over the numerous other tablets available on the market? It should not kill your spirits that a version of your idea is already available. Instead, it simply means that you must go back to the drawing board and find another way to connect A to B because using a straight line from A to B has already been done.

Do you know what category your app will fall under? (In case you do not know, you choose the category for your app once you upload it to the app store for review.) If you know the app you want to develop will be a photo app, research the apps already in the photo category in the app store. What apps are ranked and have consistently been ranked? What kind of apps or features of apps are people willing to pay for? You can find that information out by simply looking at the top paid and top grossing apps in the photo category. While searching through material, find out what stats say about the photo category. Is it the most competitive category? Is it the most popular category? Things like this may seem small, but it can be a big deal. In the case that you have an app that could fit in two different categories, such the Social Networking category or the Photo & Video category, you want to make a sound business decision on which category you should go with. You may want to go with the category that is less competitive or the category that gets the most views. This is a key decision for your app because ranked apps see additional traction simply being they are ranked.

Find Your Niche

In the previous chapter, I told you that you should search the market and know how much competition you are up against. If you feel that you have a fair chance to compete with the few apps that are similar to yours, the next step is to find your niche. What makes your app different? What service(s) are you going to offer in addition to or different from your competitor? It may not be a major difference in service, but the UI/UX (user interface and user experience) may be what you focus on. Take the time to not only ask yourself, but others, "Why would you download this app versus that app?" In fact, I wouldn't even mention that it was your app when asking others about why they would use your version versus a competitor's version. Sometimes friends do not want to hurt your feelings or will sugarcoat things simply because you are their friend. While you always want their love and support, in a moment like this, what you need more than anything is their honesty.

In regards to finding that key niche, I will use a popular example to better help you understand. How many of you had a Myspace account? I'm sure over half of you reading this book did, unless you're under the age of 25. It was one of the largest social networks at one time. We would all take the time to customize our profile, add the latest music, and encourage others to join so that we could be friends with more people than just Myspace's Tom. In the height of its prime, I'm sure no one thought that Myspace would be going anywhere or at least not anywhere anytime soon. However, after some time, a group of young college kids that were not intimidated by Myspace came along. Although they also wanted to launch a social network, they had a niche. They were going to create a social network strictly for Ivy League schools. Does anybody remember when Facebook first started at Harvard and you had to have a harvard.edu email to even sign up? That was where "The Facebook" found its niche. Of course, it went on to grow and become what is now the largest social network ever. But you don't have to start out trying to be the next Facebook. Facebook didn't start out with the goal of being the largest social network ever. They started with the niche of being a social network for Harvard students. Find your niche and go from there. With the right strategy, everything else will fall into place.

App Functionality

Once you have written down your original idea, I am certain you will make adjustments after doing your research and taking a good look at the market and your competitors. That piece of paper where you jotted down your app idea probably has random notes written everywhere on it and needs to be cleaned up. You now need to organize everything based on how you want your app to function.

Your original idea was probably very broad. Now it is time to break things down into full details. What are the functions and features you are planning for your app to have? Break those down. Use bullet points if that helps. On the next page, you will see an example based on version 2 of my app PicSlit.

* The app will have four different options for slitting a photo:
- Option 1: 3 slits
- Option 2: 6 slits
- Option 3: 9 slits
- Option 4: 12 slits

* 3 menu options
- Option 1: Upgrade
- available in the free version only
- Option 2: Restore
- this is so that users who have already paid for the upgrade but had to download the app again can easily go back to their paid status.
- Option 3: Preview
- I want to allow users to see how the app works in the case they are unsure.

Sketch Things Out

Raise your hand (I know I can't see whether you do or not) if the first thought that came to your mind after reading *sketch things out* was "I can't draw?" Guess what? That is perfectly okay. You are roughly sketching out your idea, not entering an art contest. When you were thinking of your idea, you were also thinking about how it would function and how it would look screen to screen. Get a piece of paper and draw that out. In the end, you will probably need to hire a UI/UX designer, but you need to give him/her something to go from if you want your idea to be brought to life in the way that way you envision it.

I would like to note that sketching out your design on a piece of paper is not the only option. There are numerous choices available to you, but I suggest you go with the option that is most comfortable for you. If you are a completely new to this world, I strongly suggest a piece of paper. If you are a little more advanced, there are design software programs available such as Photoshop or Sketch.

Flow Chart

The flow chart is a combination of your app functionality and your app designs. This is the longest yet **most important** part of the process. If you half-ass it with your flow-chart, you will find yourself wasting time and money once you hire a developer. If you are unsure about certain aspects of the app, you writing out the functionality and sketching out your screen designs will reveal your holes. Your job is to figure out where the holes are and fill them in. If you allow a developer to get started while you are still unsure about things, your developer will also be unsure and it will cause the app development process to take longer than expected.

Take a look at a flow chart below:

(Image via www.pinterest.com*)*

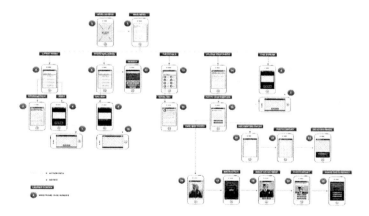

Your flow chart should show your sketches and depict how one screen will flow to the next. However, you need to show more than just the sketches. Write out what each screen does. Write the description as if you are explaining it to a five-year-old. If you sketch out a button written on **screen 1** that reads "Next," you need to explain what happens when the user taps that button. Maybe it takes the user to **screen 2** or maybe it means something different. Don't assume it's intuitive for your users. It may seem like common sense to you, but the idea also came from you.

Find a Developer

One of the most frequently asked questions from aspiring developers is, "How did you find your first developer for your app?" Many people get discouraged because they do not know how to code or because they can't find a technical co-founder, but you are not out of luck. If you are waiting around to find the perfect technical co-founder, you may never get your app created. There is a reason that freelancer developers exist. Take advantage of these freelance websites:

www.Guru.com
www.Upwork.com
www.Freelancer.com
www.Elance.com

I have personally used Guru.com and Upwork.com (formerly known as oDesk.com) to find developers for my apps when I was first starting out.

You have probably heard horror stories about freelance developers. Unfortunately, those stories do exist and most are true. Even if you find someone you think is a good fit, there are steps you should take before actually hiring a developer and paying him or her any money. I have been there and I have come across bad freelancer app developers myself, so my advice comes from the mistakes I made and that I hope to help you avoid. Do the following:

1. Read the reviews that the developer has received from past clients. If a freelancer does not have any reviews, it may be due to the fact that he or she is new to that freelance website. It does not automatically mean they are unqualified. However, if this is your first time hiring a developer, I suggest going with someone who does have reviews because you want to see testimonials of his or her work from others who have been in the same position as you. However, even with reviews, you must be cautious. First, some freelancers beg clients to leave them five star reviews. This is not fair to future clients because those reviews may not be true to the work that was done. You should not only pay attention to the reviews, but also the job for which they received the review. For example, if a developer has received three 5-star reviews but they are for jobs that cost $50 and were super simple jobs such as "Add new splash screen," then those reviews are not a true testament for the full development of an app like you are looking for.

2. Do not just base your decision solely on the reviews that have been given by past clients. Pay close attention to the portfolio of the developer. If you are looking to get a photo app done and the freelancer you are most interested in hiring has only developed two apps, both finance apps, you might want to keep looking for another developer. Some developers can develop anything you throw

their way. Others specialize in the development of a certain type of app.

3. Developers have and will falsify their portfolio. Ask for the names of past clients to do a reference check. Give those references a call or send them an e-mail. Ask as many questions as you can think of. However, don't stop there. You are spending your hard-earned money, so you have the right to make sure you are being smart with your hire. Pick two or three apps listed in the developer's portfolio and send those creators or companies an e-mail or give them a call. I have done it plenty of times without letting the potential hire know about it. I once e-mailed a company whose app the developer had in his portfolio and received an email back that said, "We have never heard of or worked with _____." It happens. Developers falsify their portfolios all the time on freelance sites. If you get one of those responses back, put a big X on that developer as a possible hire because you would probably be walking into trouble and about to just give money away.

4. Sign a non-disclosure agreement (NDA) with your chosen developer. They develop multiple apps a year and may have no interest in stealing your idea, but you can never be too sure. The downside to all of this is that you are more than likely outsourcing your development to someone in India or Pakistan and a US-based NDA probably won't do you any good if something goes south.

40

So you have found a developer. Now you are concerned about being scammed or not getting the results that you want. I have two suggestions that will help with this.

1. ALWAYS do milestone payments.

    Never pay all the money upfront. By this, I mean do not send the developer all of the money for the project before it begins. It is okay and suggested that you deposit the entire amount of money into escrow, but do not release all of the money at once to the actual developer. Having the money in escrow gives security to both you and the developer. For you, you know that if things do not go as planned with the developer, you can receive your money back. It may not be an easy process if the developer decides to fight you on this, but it is better in escrow than in the developer's bank account when he or she is no longer responding to your calls or emails. For developers, it decreases the chance of you not paying for their service. The money is in escrow. It may not be released to them yet, but the money is where they can see it and be assured you aren't going to rip them off.

2. Do a contract with your developer and be sure to state in your contract that ALL codes and any additional material dealing with your app will

belong to you after you have made the final payment.

You will need your codes in case you want to hire another developer when it is time to update your app. You also need these codes because, quite simply, you paid for them.

Test Your App

There are some companies who charge thousands of dollars to test your app. There is no need to fork over that much money for your first, simple app.

A. Your developer will test the app out as they are developing it, but the developers are not perfect. Some are lazy and do not spend a lot of time testing after they have completed coding. Other times, the developer may test the app thoroughly, but still miss errors in the functionality of the app.

B. Test your own app. Depending on how complex the app is, you can ask the developer to send you a version to test after each milestone. Even with the developer testing it, you will catch bugs that he or she will not. Plus, you know more than anyone else on how the app is supposed to function. Write down all bugs and communicate with your developer to get them fixed.

C. Testflight, the Apple service you use to test out your app, allows you to add multiple tester accounts. All you need is the email of the people you want to test our your app. For Android, you send out your APK file to those you want to test your app. I suggest allowing at least five people to test your app before you release it.

To test out your iOS app, the people you want to test your app must download the TestFlight app first. The app is free.

I know that you are excited about your app. I know that you are ready to get your app in the App Store, but do not let that stop you from being a critical tester of your app. If the app crashes, note it. If the app is not functioning exactly how you want it to, note it. If the design of the app does not look how you designed it or envisioned it, note it. Let your developer know of every single issue/error/bug that you find in the app when you are testing it.

The best way to minimize encountering many errors all at once is to do milestones. As a beginner, testing an app with lots of bugs can be overwhelming. By testing per milestone completion, you are testing your app in steps and not all at once.

Bugs can be missed or not noticed in the beginning so be sure that before hiring a developer that you have a contract outlining a warranty period. I would suggest that this warranty period be a minimum of 60 days. That way, if the users who have downloaded your app inform you of bugs in your app that you and/or the developer missed, the developer must fix those bugs. The warranty period does not cover new features, but instead is used to correct bugs that are in the existing, original coding.

Let a friend or even a complete stranger use your app while you watch. Everything may seem like it should be easy to use to you, but remember that it is your idea and it came from your head, not your users' head. If they have trouble figuring it out, make the needed adjustments for a better user experience (UX).

Your Developer Account

Another question that I am often asked is, "How exactly does your app get into the app store?" For those of you who have the same question, this chapter will be the answer you have been searching for.

Successfully getting your app developed is just one part of the journey. Making it available for the world to download is another part. One good thing about hiring freelancers is that most will upload your app to the App Store for you at your request, though you will have to provide them with all of the necessary information and details.

First things first, you need to create a developer account. You need to do this personally, not your hired freelancer. The account you create is determined by whether you have an iOS or Android application.

If you are having an iOS (iPhone, iPad) mobile app developed, you will need to visit https://developer.apple.com/programs/. You will need to choose the option of iOS developer when asked what program you are interested in enrolling. Apple has a separate developer program for Mac apps and other programs so make sure you choose the correct option. The developer fee for iOS is $99 per year. There is no way around this. You must have a developer account in order to have your app(s) made available to download in the Apple App Store.

If you are developing an app for Android, you will need to visit https://play.google.com/apps/publish/ to create an account. Unlike the $99 per year fee for Apple, Google only charges a one-time $25 fee.

You will have to choose between enrolling as an individual or enrolling as an organization. If you enroll as an organization, you must have a D-U-N-S Numbers, must be a legal entity (meaning you must have filed your company as an LLC, INC., or whatever option you decide to go with), a bank account, and your EIN (employer identification number). Your EIN is a nine-digit number assigned by the IRS. You get your EIN number at https://www.irs.gov/businesses/small-businesses-self-employed/apply-for-an-employer-identification-number-ein-online.

Once you have successfully created your developer account and agreed to all the terms & agreements, you now have to upload your app for review. In the process of uploading your app or getting your freelancer to upload your app, you will have to know or provide the following information:

A.   *Name of your app*
The name you choose for your app can be the difference maker. You have two options. First, and perhaps most obviously, you can name your app to describe exactly what it does. For

example, I have an app called Words on Pics. Can you guess what it does? Hard one? Right! The app allows you to add words on pictures. However, some apps have created a brand name that isn't intuitive, but is still successful. An example of this would be Instagram. Instagram has a meaning now that didn't exist 20 years ago. Before the release of the app, if you had heard the word Instagram, you would have never thought of a media social network that allows you to share picture and videos.

B. *Keywords*

Think about your keywords carefully. What keywords best describe your app? What keywords do you feel should show your app in the search results? Think about what word or phrase you would search for if you were hoping to find your app. Pick the top keywords and add those to the keyword section for your app in your developer account.

I suggest using services to assist you with looking at keywords that your competitors are using, volume number, and hit count. You can use free services like www.Searchman.com to help you with this.

C.   *Description of your app*

This is where you are going to describe your app to your potential customers. Be specific. Be to the point. You will want to inform your potential app users of how the app works, the features of your app, what makes it cool, and any other helpful information. Try to convince someone within the first two or three sentences of your description that your app is the app they have been searching for. Trust me, that will be all they will read before they decide yes or no on downloading your app.

D.   *Category*

Choose the category that is the best fit for your app. Does your app allow people to edit photos? If so, Photo & Video will be the category you choose. Is your app a game? Then you will choose Games. You will have the choice of a primary and secondary category.

E.   *App rating*

Does your app contain violence, nudity, gambling, etc.? You will rate your app by answering yes or no questions. Your app may be for everyone or only for a mature crowd. Your rating will determine this and will be shown when someone goes to look at your app in the app store.

F.   *App icon*

Just as I mentioned how important your app name is, so is your app icon. It is your identifier. It is what people will associate with your app. You want an app icon that is eye-catching. If someone is searching for an app and they are scrolling through to see which app they want to look more into, they are more than likely going to click on the one with the most appealing app icon and screenshots.

G.   *Screenshots*

Screenshots of your app is probably the most *underrated,* yet important piece of your app description. You think no one cares about your screenshots? That would be a lie. People look at those screenshots to see how the app works and what the app offers. In fact, many people skip completely over the written description of the app and make their decision to download the app or not based completely on the screenshots available.

Do not just throw something together because you are overly anxious to get your app in the App Store. Each of these pieces could play a role in your position and the success of your app. But never forget that the quality of your app itself will determine if the person that downloads your app continues to use your app.

Once you have done your part, you can now only sit back, bite your nails, and wait on the verdict from the App Store, whether it is Apple, Android (Google), or another app store. The time limit of the review process varies.

For Apple, they have made a commitment to try to get reviews done within 48 hours, but do not freak out if it takes a little longer. You truly never know. Once it is reviewed, you will find out if your app has been approved or rejected. If the app is approved, it will become available in the App Store and people will be able to download and enjoy your app. If it is rejected, Apple will inform you why your app was rejected. Do not panic. Maybe it was because of too many bugs in the app causing it to not work properly. Maybe your app had some material that was copyrighted. Rejection can be for any number of reasons, but whatever the reason may be, send the reason of rejection to your developer, have the developer correct the issue, and re-upload your app for approval. If you feel that you have been rejected in error, you do have the right to appeal the decision.

For Android, once you have uploaded your app to your developer console, it takes about 30 minutes to two hours to become available in the Google Play Store. The review process is not as rigorous for Android as it is for

Apple. However, your app can still be removed from the Google Play Store for violations.

The possibility of rejection is the reason I suggest that you make the final milestone of payment to your developer after the approval of your app. If you pay before approval, some developers may feel that because they now have all of their money, they can take their precious time in making the corrections to your rejected app. However, if the developer knows that the final payment will not be released until the approval of the app, I can guarantee you that the developer wants the approval of your app just as much as you do and will work quickly to get errors fixed.

Monitor Your Progress

Pay attention to the feedback from your customers. Read every review left about your app. Read and respond to each email that is sent to you about your app. Do not only read the feedback, but also react to the feedback. If 90 of the 100 emails or reviews you receive about your app are saying, "This app is good, but it needs more color options," you need to take this into consideration and think about adding more color options.

In monitoring your progress, do not get discouraged if you find yourself with less than 5 star reviews. While the goal is to create and provide a quality app, you will never make every customer happy. The point of monitoring your progress and your reviews is not to change every little thing someone complains about because you are then fighting a losing battle. However, you do want to pay attention to feedback and complaints when numerous customers mention the same thing.

Changes and Updates

It is guaranteed that you will need to make changes and have updates to your app. Users will know if you have developed an app and then abandoned it. This probably means that they won't download it. Three of the most common reasons that you will have to make changes and/or updates are:

A. *Bugs*
>   This can include your app crashing, inactive links, etc.

B. *User Feedback*
>   As mentioned previously, pay close attention to your feedback. They will request or point out things that you and/or your team missed during testing. No worries. Just take the time to go in, make changes and submit the update to the app store.

C. *Market and/or Software Change*
>   The mobile app market changes so quickly and you must keep up with it if you plan to give your app a fighting chance. This also includes software changes. If you are developing an iOS app, you have to take into consideration

all the changes and adjustments developers must make when Apple goes from iOS 9 to iOS 10. The update in software usually happens every year, so always take note of the changes and consider how you can better take advantage of them and get out ahead of the curve.

As a developer, you will have early access to software updates. For example, if iOS 10 will be made available to be public on September 19, 2017, Apple will allow you access to beta versions of iOS 10 in advance so that you can prepare your apps for the update.

Part 3
My Suggestions & Tips

Mobile Applications

Tip #1

You don't have to attempt to hit a home run with your first app. You can do a simple and cost-friendly app. My first app cost me $3,500. I was in college and asked my dad to loan me the money, which he did. My second app, Words on Pics, cost less to develop than my first app.

Many times, freelance developers or companies will try to charge you thousands upon thousands of dollars to develop your app. This mostly happens to people who have no clue that they are being taken advantage of. Take it from me when I say that it is possible to get a quality app developed without paying $50,000 for it.

Tip #2

You have two choices when you are naming your app.

1. It is highly recommended that you name your app something that describes what the app does. I will use the popular game Hill Climb Racing as an example. The name of the game also describes the action of the game. You want people to be able to find your app easily when searching the App Store for an app they want. If you name your app "The Checkbook" when a person who wants a checkbook app searches the App Store by typing

in the keyword 'checkbook,' the name of your app alone has increased the chances of your app showing near the top of the search results.

2. You can name your app a new word or a name that does not have a direct reflection of the functionality of the app. The example I will use here is my first app, PAMO. Nothing about the word PAMO tells you that the app was a checkbook app. One positive of making up a name versus using a descriptive name is that it adds value and branding to your app. Another example of this would be the once popular app, Vine. If you mention the word vine, most people will think of a plant that has very long stems. However, for those that are familiar with the social media world of today, Vine has a different meaning. Ten years ago, no one would have connected the word Vine to a media social network of six-second videos.

Tip #3

You must make a decision on whether or not you want your app to be a free, paid, blended model, freemium, premium, or a subscription based. As of today, freemium models account for over 70% of the revenue made with apps. Freemium is a great option because people are able to download your app for free, but they must pay for certain features. Think about Candy Crush. The app is completely free, but many of us are guilty of buying some in-app purchase.

A big consideration when it comes to your decision to do a free app, paid app, or one of the other models is if you want to make money now, make money later or make money at all. If this is an app for your business, you may make the app free because you're not trying to make money from the app itself. Instead, you are just trying to give your customers better and more convenient access to schedule an appointment, view events or interact with your business in other ways.

On the other hand, you may be creating an app that you want to focus on gaining traction and building the largest community possible in the early stages of your company. In this case, you will go with making your app free, but looking for a pay day later. Think about Instagram. Instagram is completely free, yet they sold to Facebook for $1 billion because they created a community of over 60 million people.

If you are planning to do a paid app because you think it is the only way to make money right now, you should be aware that it is not. You can have a free app, but include ads from third party sources like AdMob, RevMob, or other similar mobile advertising platforms.

Tip #4

Oh, the importance of numbers. I will give a quick run-down of two numbers in this section: (1) Profit and (2) Downloads.

Profit

Understanding how you make money with paid apps is important. If you are selling an app for $0.99, you are not profiting $0.99. You are instead profiting 70% of $0.99 and Apple or Google (Android) is profiting 30%. So yes, even after you have paid a developer to develop your app and paid for a developer account, you are still not making 100% of the profit from your paid app, in-app purchase, etc. Sounds crazy, huh? But do not get me wrong, 70% is better than nothing. And in the long run – or possibly the short run - that 70% can be quite profitable for you.

Downloads

You will be able to see your downloads every morning (though sometimes the report is delayed). The sales report will inform you of the number of downloads your app received from the previous day. You can see this by logging into iTunes Connect or your Google Play developer console.

Usually your download numbers will look great the first few days your app becomes available in the App Store.

Your friends are downloading it, your co-workers are downloading it, and because it is new people from all over are downloading it just to see what the app is about. Not to sound harsh, but do not let this boost your ego too high. A large number of downloads happens for a lot of people when their app is first released. If your numbers are still looking impressive after a few weeks of your app being available, you may have something special on your hands. If the numbers of downloads have dropped dramatically, do not think that something terribly wrong has happened. It is actually quite normal. In fact, over half of the apps in the app stores are considered zombie apps, meaning they have either never been downloaded or only downloaded a few times.

Tip #5

If you have spent all of your money on the development of your app, you can still do free marketing. But let me be clear, while it may be free as far as money, it is not free in the sense of time. You can easily pay a public relations or marketing company to do all the work for you or you can take the time to do it yourself.

Social media is a key marketing tool to take advantage of. You should be creating profiles on Twitter, Facebook, Instagram, Snapchat, and Pinterest. There are millions of people on social networks and it gives you the opportunity to reach more of your potential customers.

Do not stop at social media. You should also do press releases. There are several sites that allow you to submit your press release for free. Submit to as many outlets as possible.

There are also numerous app review sites available. While some may charge a small fee, there are numerous sites that do not. If you have a paid app, you will need to provide the review site with a promo code. You are given 50 promo codes with each new version of your app. Use those 50 available promo codes wisely.

In the case that you do have a small budget to spend on advertising, spend responsibly and try not to spend all of your money in one place. Find out what works for you because what worked for another app company may not work for you. You need to find your niche, know your audience, and find the best way to get your app in front of those people. If this means getting pens made and passing them out around a college campus, so be it. If you want to create a video that you hope goes viral, do it. It does not take a big budget to create a big buzz.

Another service I would recommend using is Fiverr. It is a marketplace that has services that start as low as $5.

Tip #6

I want to make sure that I also give you the reality of this business. In my mind, I knew that my first app was the best idea ever. I was not worried about advertising or anything else. I knew that the idea was so great that as soon as it hit the App Store and became available to download, it would get thousands and thousands of downloads and sooner rather than later, I would be rich. I was wrong.

There are over a million apps available in the Apple App Store and Google Play Store. With that being said, reality sets in quickly. Let me type that again. There are millions of apps available in the app stores. Although fewer apps were available when I released PAMO, it still wasn't a walk in the park. PAMO did not sell or get the downloads that I had expected it to get. Yes, it hurt my personal feelings but not my business feelings. Why? Because in the business world, you will hear the word "no" far more than you will hear the word "yes". You have to learn to accept failure. It is part of the process. Accept that small defeat, learn from it, improve, and work on creating your next project.

Networking

When I first started Sheena Allen Apps in mid-2011, I did not care about anyone knowing my name. Of course my company was named after me, but it really wasn't a marketing tactic at first. I named it Sheena Allen Apps because I couldn't think of anything else at the time. The first three years of being in business, I had achieved a massive amount of traction, but had done very little networking. Between 2011 and 2013, I may have attended five networking events. Due to being new to the entrepreneurship world and originally wanting to stay behind the scenes and just make money without being in the spotlight, I did not put myself out there to meet and network with those that I should have been trying to get to know. I did not understand the power and importance of networking early on. That all changed after meeting Anthony Frasier and having a conversation in December 2014 with Wayne Sutton. Trust me when I say that networking is key. Your network will contribute to your net worth.

Tip #1

"There is a thin line between networking and using."
- Paul C. Brunson

It is not networking if every time you reach out to someone it is to ask for a favor. Networking is about

66

building relationships, not about using. It should never be the case if you send a message to John, John knows the minute he receives your email that you are going to be asking for something. Once this becomes the case, John will eventually start to ignore your calls and emails.

I keep up with the people I have met along the way through social media or e-mail. I send e-mails to give an update on my progress, ask how his or her progress is going on a particular project, or just check in. As a millennial, I can say that our generation walks a fine line between networking and using, but know that networking will take you places that using never will. Be patient and build a solid relationship before asking for that big favor or to be connected.

Tip #2

When are you are asking someone to connect you with someone else, make sure that you are ready for that introduction. You need to network to build up the trust so that whoever you ask to make an introduction for you, they know you and your project well enough that they do not hesitate.

Also, understand that when someone makes an introduction on your behalf, the person they are connecting you with will look more at who is making the connection versus looking at you. For example, I may have known Sarah for three years and have witnessed her build her startup to over a million dollars in revenue and 5 full time employees. I have networked with Sara, shared advice, and know how hard she works. If Sarah makes an introduction on your behalf and she requests that I take a look at your app because it is the next big thing, I am more likely to stop what I am doing and look at what you have in the works. However, what you have to consider is that if I take a look at your project and it is not up to par and a waste of my time, I do not blame you. I am going to put the blame on Sarah. With that being said, if someone is hesitate or refuses to make an introduction for you, it probably has nothing to do with that person being a butthole. It is more likely that you may need to get your project together before it is time for that introduction.

Tip #3

Be sure to attend conferences and other business gatherings. You will be able to meet many like-minded people by attending different conferences. I usually don't go to conferences to hear the speakers. I go to meet the other people that are attending because most are eager to build relationships just like I am.

You can find conferences that fit your interest by searching websites like Eventbrite and Meetup. I would also recommend setting up Google alerts for networking events that interest you.

Tip #4

You never know whom you are sitting beside or in the room with. Closed mouths don't get fed. Talk to people. It doesn't have to be in an aggressive manner, but it can be done in a professional way. Investors are not going to always be in a suit or have a shirt on that says, "Hi, I'm an investor." The connector in the room may be the quietest in the room. The only way you can know who you are in the room with and the potential of magic that can happen with the person you are around is by networking with them.

Tip #5

Always be mindful of the type of event you are attending. There are times that I will purposely not bring business cards. For me, small networking events means I'm not bringing business cards, but a large reworking event means I'm bringing plenty of them. Smaller events are more intimate and you really want to be able to get to know the people in the room, not just hand them a business card and hope that he or she emails you. It's not a grab and go situation. Larger events may be different because things are moving faster. You don't want to miss out on potentially connecting with someone so if you only have time to run up and pass off a business card, do so.

Mentors

If no one has informed you, mentors are vital to your journey.

Tip #1

I am often asked how to find a mentor. It is not as hard as it may seem. Find someone you would like to be your mentor and ask. There are so many ways to get in contact with people now, whether it be their personal or business website or their social media profiles. Of course you have to be realistic about this. If you tweet Kanye West and ask him to mentor you, you will probably not get a response. However, look at those that are up-and-coming and have seen success and can be helpful to you as you start your journey to try to get to where your potential mentor is.

Know that the person you reach out to can only give you a yes or no if you ask them to be your mentor. If the person doesn't respond or says no, move on to the next potential mentor. Don't take it personally and don't stop looking.

Tip #2

It is important to have mentors both in your industry and outside of your industry. The majority of my mentors are in the tech space, but I also have mentors that are in the entertainment industry, fashion industry, and real estate. This is vital because it allows for you to get different perspectives.

Tip #3

Appreciate your mentors. The majority of us are guilty of taking things and people for granted. There could be hundreds of other people hoping to be mentored by the mentor you are blessed to have. Your mentor is like your accountability partner. You must show that you can and will do the work and that you are worthy of your mentor giving his or her time, making connections or potentially even investing money.

Raising Money

Tip #1

Go to your family and friends first to help get your company off the ground. I know for some people this option is a complete no-go, but if is possible, make it your first option.

Tip #2

Bootstrap when it is possible. As you grow and want to scale, you will more than likely find yourself raising outside funds, but bootstrap as long as you can. Bootstrapping means that you are using your own money to grow your company. This is not easy for most, but there is beauty in bootstrapping. One, you are able to do things at your own pace. You do not have to answer to investors. Two, you are able to retain ownership of your company. Once you start bringing in investors, you have to start giving up equity in your company and your baby becomes less and less yours.

Tip #3

Many people want to run to an investor when they have an idea. That is not the way the process works. No investor wants to write you a check if you have nothing to show for the business other than an idea. How much money have you invested? What does your team look like? What is your market size? How much traction and/or revenue does the company have? All of these things matter. If you are lucky enough to land an investor off just an idea, they will more than likely require a large percentage of your company because they feel you are high-risk.

Tip #4

Take advantage of all of the fundraising options that are available now. Investors are not the only way to raise money anymore. Check out different incubators and accelerators. Accelerators can be idea stage or growth stage. Also, look into crowdfunding. Crowdfunding allows you to raise money in exchange for a perk to those early donors and customers. Another option is to look for strategic partnerships. Find someone who has a strength where you are weak and find a way to work together that benefits both parties.

Tip #5

I have witnessed entrepreneurs not want to present to investors unless the investor signed a confidentiality agreement. While it is great to take protective measures of your idea or company, most investors are pitched to every single day. An investor's job is to find great companies and invest in them to help them scale and eventually exit. Investors are not in the business to steal ideas. If the only thing keeping you from pitching to a potential investor is the fact that he or she will not sign a non-disclosure agreement, being an entrepreneur may not be the career for you.

The Why - Part II

Being an entrepreneur is not easy. It looks really great in the news headlines when you see entrepreneurs making millions of dollars, making their own schedule, and enjoying life on a different level than the average person. However, it takes a special person to be an entrepreneur because in order to get to all those perks, it takes sacrifices, failures, and times of doubt.

The only person that knows if you have what it takes to be an entrepreneur is you. It doesn't matter if you come from a family of entrepreneurs or if you are the first one. If the magic is in you, it's meant to be. Never allow the odds against you to stop you from pursuing entrepreneurship. Why? Entrepreneurship is not a one-size fits all. We do not all look the same, think the same, act the same, or come from the same background. Why? Because we are humans creating companies to serve billions of people with different needs and different likes. What you have to find is your niche. You have to find what you are going to do to impact others. You have to find out who you are. One of my favorite songs is Everything I Am by Kanye West. In the song he raps:

"Everything I'm not, made me everything I am"
- Kanye West

Use what makes you different to your benefit. Use what you understood that others may not and disrupt an industry. That is what entrepreneurship is all about.

Cheers to taking the leap of faith.

Trust the Struggle.
Trust the Journey.

Be You.
Be the Change.